Series title: **BLACK LEADERS IN THE FREEDOM STRUGGLE**

TOUSSAINT

L'OUVERTURE

by Marie Stuart

Illustrated by Deborah Weymont

This book is part of a series written by Marie Stuart (Tyrwhitt) and published in her memory.

Marie wanted stories about the lives of these brave people to be more widely known. She believed that such stories would serve to encourage those facing the same challenges today.

Published in 1993 Central and East Bristol Adult Continuing Education Centre, © with the sponsorship of relatives, friends and colleagues of Marie Tyrwhitt.

Reprinted in 1998 by Marie Tyrwhitt Publications©, at Bristol Community Education Service, Stoke Lodge Centre, Shirehampton Road, Stoke Bishop, Bristol BS9 1BN.

Reprinted 2002

Printed by Printing & Stationery Services, UWE, Bristol.

Marie Stuart, the author of the books in the Black Leaders in the Freedom Struggle series, was a teacher of adults and children and a writer throughout all her long life. She was also a learner and one who believed that to be really alive means to be growing and changing. To do so means that we must be free. Free to question and free to find our own answers and our own way.

Marie Stuart wrote these books out of a passion for freedom for all, regardless of race, colour or creed, and out of a deep admiration for the heroes celebrated in this series. They are 'heroes' not because they conquered great empires, but because, by their actions and their example, they gave something of great value to the liberation of their people. They stood up and took their place proudly amongst the human race, having struggled heroically against the disadvantages to which they were born. These stories and those lives will never die as long as we have the courage to strive for our human right to dignity and equality and the generosity to realise that the breath of freedom is sharing. It is in that spirit that these books should be read and in loyalty to the memory of those brave black leaders in our freedom struggle.

TOUSSAINT L'OUVERTURE
Chapter 1
Toussaint - the Slave

On May 20th, 1744, a boy was born in the French part of the Island of St. Dominigue (now called Haiti - the other half was Spanish). His parents were both black. They worked in the sugar plantation of Bréda. The child was given the French name of Toussaint (Too-san). He had no surname at that time. His father had been a king of the Arcadas tribe in Africa, but he had been captured in a tribal war and sold to a slave merchant who shipped him to the West Indies.

When Toussaint was small, his father used to talk to him in his native tongue and tell him stories about Africa. Sometimes he would dance and sing folk songs. This made Toussaint feel that Africa was his real home.

The man who had bought Toussaint's father was a French Count. Unlike the owners of many plantations, he would not let his slaves be whipped. He treated Toussaint's father with respect and gave him freedom within the bounds of the estate. He also kept an eye on Toussaint as he could see that the boy was very intelligent. He even arranged for him to be taught to read by one of the Catholic priests. Later he lent him some of his own books, so Toussaint was able to read books by famous people. He was grateful for this and never forgot the kindness shown towards him.

However, he never forgot the Sunday when, as he was coming out of church, a white man came up and beat him over the head with his stick. Why? Because he, a black slave boy, *dared* to be reading a prayer book. Toussaint's coat was splashed with blood. He never wore it again but kept it as a reminder. It taught him that the secret of the white man's power over the black lay in education. That was why the white man did not want the black man to read books. Books gave ideas. Toussaint kept these ideas in his mind and thought about them. He liked being alone because the other boys could not read and were not aware of these things.

Toussaint was small for his age. He was only five feet two inches tall as a grown man. He made up for his lack of height by being good at climbing, swimming, jumping, running and so on. Best of all he loved horse-riding. In this he was encouraged by his master for it was important to have someone on the estate who could ride well. In those days there were no telephones, and letters took a long time to come, so messages were taken by a rider on horseback. As soon as he was old enough, the Count made Toussaint his postilion. This meant that he drove the carriage seated on one of the horses. He loved this job because it gave him more freedom to see and hear what was happening in the world outside the plantation. Some of the things he saw made him very sad and angry, such as slaves being whipped on many of the estates. He knew that he was lucky to have a more lenient master.

Often he had to ride to the big city called Le Cap. It was a port and there were always ships from overseas anchored in the harbour. If he had time, he would stop on the quay and talk to the sailors who came from France. That part of St. Dominigue was then a French colony. France was a long way off but Toussaint was interested to hear about what was happening there. And a lot *was* happening, for these were the days leading up to the French Revolution. Toussaint kept on hearing the words, 'Freedom', 'Equality', 'Liberty'. Someone called Tom Paine had written a book, "The Rights of Man." Toussaint wished he could get hold of that book. It was all very interesting and exciting. The young man listened and remembered, but he was a slave and, as yet, there was nothing he could do about it.

In fact he enjoyed his work. He was now promoted to being head stockman, and in charge of the stables. He was always good with animals and looked after them well. He had learned a lot about herbs from his mother before she had died. She had taught him how to use them as medicine for curing some sicknesses. Toussaint was a natural 'healer' and the other slaves used to come to him as their doctor.

His final position was as a coachman on the estate. His duty now was to drive his master and mistress to visit other plantations. Here he could go into the big houses - not, of course, as a guest. He could see how the rich people behaved. He could catch glimpses of them dancing in the ballrooms, see how they dressed and listen to how they spoke to each other in Parisian French.

He could also hear the talk of the other slaves in the kitchens where he had to wait - how one had been whipped for breaking a dish, or burning a cake, or letting the baby cry at night and waking its mother, her mistress. He soon found out that many masters and mistresses did not treat their slaves in the same way that his master treated him.

At other times he would have to drive his master to his Club. While waiting there he would hear more talk about politics and the new ideas. Of course he could not join in, and only heard bits of what they were saying through an open window or door. But the words Liberty, Freedom and Equality kept cropping up - and that man Tom Paine and his "Rights of Man" was often spoken about. Now more than ever Toussaint wished he could read that book.

So the days and months passed by and he was now almost forty years of age. Time to get married - indeed, he had left it rather late! Not that he had not been attracted by pretty women, or they by him, in spite of his small stature, but marriage was a different thing. He wanted a wife who would be good at looking after the home and the children - when they came. So he chose Suzanne Baptiste, the daughter of his godfather. She was not very pretty but she was gentle and kind and a comfortable person to live with. She was about thirty-five when they married. Toussaint was always very fond of her. He loved her in much the same way as he had loved his mother. During the next ten years they had three children, who were all boys. Toussaint continued working as a trusted headman on a large plantation.

Chapter 2

After the Slave Revolt, Toussaint becomes Leader

At that time most masters treated their slaves with shocking brutality. Some slaves ran away and hid in the mountains in the north of the island. Here they lived by hunting and fishing in much the same way as they would have lived in Africa. But they could not go back to Africa and they hated the whites who had taken them from their native land and made them slaves. They hated them for separating them from their wives and for all the suffering they had had to endure.

One of these men was a slave who had escaped from the nearby island of Jamaica. This man, like Toussaint, had met men from the outside world and heard them talking about what was going on there. He also had heard those magic words Liberty, Freedom and Equality. He asked himself questions and thought about slavery when he was alone in the mountains. He saw that slavery was due to the white man's greed. He felt it was wrong of the slaves to submit to it. They should stand up for themselves. They must refuse to be downtrodden. If they all banded together they could get rid of the whites and be free. He had heard that there were at least fifteen times as many blacks as whites on the island. He talked to some of the other runaways about it. Some who heard him were afraid of being recaptured, tortured and killed. Others agreed with him but asked what they could do. The whites had an army with soldiers, and ammunition sent from France. The plantation owners all had guns. They, the slaves, were unarmed and they were helpless. Not if they acted together, he replied. He would be their leader and tell them what to do. They must have a plan. They must take the whites by surprise and act quickly. Two of the men agreed with him and said they would help him lead the revolt.

It began on August 14th, 1791. It was a Sunday evening, the one day in the week when all the slaves would be at home and not working in the fields. The three leaders raced on horseback from one plantation to another, urging the slaves to action. They told them that they must murder their masters and mistresses while they slept. How? with knives, stones, axes, or by strangling them with their bare hands. Their hate would give them the strength. They must remember all the suffering they had put up with and take their revenge.

The word spread like wild fire from mouth to mouth. Yes, fire! That was their weapon. They must set fire to everything. The sugar canes in the plantations blazed like an inferno. The masters' houses went up in flames. The masters awoke from sleep and tried to escape but were hacked down without mercy, strangled, or beaten to death. Now they were paying the price for years of their brutality. Even those who had treated their slaves well were not spared. If they had a white skin they must go.

'Destroy! Destroy!' came the orders, 'Burn everything!' Soon the whole countryside was ablaze. The factories with the sugar boilers were blackened ruins. The broken machinery made deadly weapons, better than their masters' guns which they didn't know how to use.

Some of the masters managed to escape on horseback. Others put their wives and children and their most valuable possessions in coaches and tried to drive off to the coast. Terror and hate raged throughout the night.

By the morning the news had got through to Le Cap, the capital of the French part of the island. The governor called out the troops. Frantic plantation owners dashed to the quay on horseback, or in their coaches, begging the captains of ships anchored in the harbour to take them and their wives and children *anywhere* - to France, Jamaica, Trinidad, the United States, anywhere to escape this inferno.

There were 100,000 slaves let loose and they were all marching to the coast! The governor ordered fortifications to be put up round the town. The cannon must be turned to face the land instead of the sea, for the enemy was now in their midst. Utter chaos was everywhere. Neither side showed mercy to the other. It was a holocaust.

In the end the guns were victors and the slaves had to retreat to the hills. But they did not give in, and it is said that in the next month ten thousand black people and two thousand white people died.

While all this was happening, what was Toussaint doing? On the night of the uprising he did not take an active part in the revolt. In return for the kindness his master had always shown him he felt he must protect him now.

So, with the help of his brother, he managed to get the whole family on board a schooner sailing for America. He also sent his own wife and children to a safe place in the Spanish part of the island.

This done, he rode off to join the rebels. Now he felt *free.* His head was held high. His heart was light. For the first time in his life, and he was nearly fifty, he felt that he was his own master. He spurred his horse to a gallop as the magic word Liberty coursed through his veins. When he arrived at the camp he found that the leaders had lost heart. The Jamaican slave who had started the rebellion had been killed, and the others were feeling lost without him. None of them could read or write, and they could not understand what was happening in France. And a lot *was* happening for the French Revolution was now in full swing.

They welcomed Toussaint because they felt that he knew about these things. Also he knew about herbs and medicines, and that was more important at the moment for the camp was full of badly wounded men in need of care and attention. The other leaders knew that Toussaint had been a sort of doctor on the estate at Bréda so they now appointed him doctor of the camp. By his gentle care of the sick and suffering he won their affection and loyalty. They looked upon him as their saviour.

When he had arrived the camp was very dirty and untidy. He knew that good health depended on cleanliness, so he set the able-bodied men to work, getting things in order. Because he had been the headman of a big plantation he knew this could not be done without discipline, and when the men saw that it was for their own good they obeyed him.

Many of the men who were not wounded were dressed up in all kinds of finery they had robbed from the big houses on the estates. Toussaint told them they looked as if they were in fancy dress at a carnival instead of soldiers fighting for their freedom. He promised that he would try to get them proper uniforms so that they would look like a real army, and he would buy guns and teach them how to shoot. He told them that now they had got their freedom they would have to fight to keep it or it would be taken away from them. In this way he turned a horde of rebels into a disciplined army.

His orders were clear and simple but had to be obeyed. First, there was to no more looting. Food could be collected from the masters' houses that had not been destroyed, but it must be brought to the camp to be shared by all since they must eat. But there was to be no more wanton damage. And no more rape - *that* was to be punished by death.

Although he was now a soldier, Toussaint hated unnecessary violence and killing. He was a man of compassion. Once, he and some of the men came upon a group of white women who had been molested and left without clothes. Toussaint dismounted, took off his cloak and threw it round one of the women. Then he ordered his men to give their jackets to the others. These women's husbands must have been killed in the revolt because they were slave owners. So the women were 'the enemy.' But now they were helpless and Toussaint did not believe in retribution.

Chapter 3

"I want Liberty and Equality to reign throughout St. Dominigue."

News of the revolt was sent to France by the Governor of Le Cap. But France was in the middle of her own revolution, and the King had been arrested and executed. Those who were now in power proclaimed that all men should be free and equal. So a commission was sent out to make peace with the slaves who had revolted in their colony of St. Dominigue. Their offer was a pardon and freedom for the *leaders.* In return they had to see to it that their followers went back to the plantations to work for their old masters as slaves.

The offer was refused. The commissioners returned to France and had second thoughts. Clearly something must be done with thousands of slaves on the loose. But what? The next man who was sent out said that *all* the slaves should be free. However, Toussaint did not trust his word. After all he was a white man and it was white men who had who had brought the slaves here from Africa. But if all men had been born free why should black men accept their freedom as a gift from the whites? A gift could be taken back by the next person sent out from France. Anyway things were in such a state of chaos there that it was difficult to know whose word could be trusted.

So Toussaint made his own proclamation in these words:

"Brothers and Friends,

I am Toussaint L'Ouverture. My name is perhaps known to you. I have undertaken to avenge you. I want liberty and equality to reign throughout St. Dominigue. I am working towards that end. Come and join me, brothers, and combat by our side for the same cause."

This was the first time Toussaint had used the name L'Ouverture. It was a French word meaning an opening or gateway. By using it he meant that he would help his fellow slaves to escape to freedom. From then he used this as his surname.

Although Toussaint had never been trained as a soldier he became a very clever general. He had read history books about men, such as Julius Caesar, who had fought campaigns. He made use now of what he had learned from this reading. But he also had ideas of his own and was the first to use small bands of men to attack by stealth. This is now called guerilla warfare.

Meanwhile other countries were watching what was happening in St. Dominigue. First Spain, who owned the nearby island of Jamaica, was afraid that their plantation slaves would start rebelling. It would be easy for slaves from St. Dominigue to make boats from their trees and row across the sea to stir up trouble.

Then there were the plantation owners who had escaped after the rebellion and fled to America, Jamaica, Spain and France. They wanted their plantations back. St.Dominigue was a very rich island. The owners had made fortunes from crops of sugar, tea, coffee and cocoa. They were not going to give this up without a fight.

So Toussaint had to expect attack from all sides. He was like a juggler trying to keep a dozen balls in the air at the same time! He was a man of great energy and needed little sleep. He was also a superb horseman, so he would dash round the island fending off attacks from all sides. His enemies never knew where he was or when he would pop up!

After the revolt there were about a hundred thousand freed slaves with Toussaint and a few other black leaders. But it was Toussaint who had to decide what must be done with them. He organised the young and able-bodied into an army. But he knew that he must get the country back on its feet again. The army needed guns and ammunition and they all needed food. This meant money to pay for it.

When he looked at the plantations that had been wrecked in the revolt, he saw that there were new green shoots pushing up through the burnt stubble. They gave him hope of recovery and told him what to do. Now he began to think as he had done when he was headman of the estate at Bréda. He saw what must be done. He must ask the slave-owners to come back, but on *his* terms!

He needed them because they had experience and knew how a plantation should be run. They knew how the sugar boilers worked. They knew who would buy sugar from them. Of course they would need workers in the plantations but they would not be slaves. They must be paid. He said that a quarter of the profit from the estate must go to the workers as wages. Another quarter was to go to the State to pay for the needs of the army, for building roads and schools and so on, and the remaining half would belong to the owners.

Some of them agreed to this and came back. Some of the ex-slaves agreed to go to work for their old masters for wages. But many did not want to go. They were happy to grow enough food for their needs on their own little plot of land as they had done in their African villages.

However, Toussaint knew that the country must produce more than for its bare needs if it was to become independent - and that is what he was aiming for. He wanted St. Dominigue to be an independent *black* nation, not a colony of *white* France. For this reason he wanted to have the money to build schools. He knew it was a lack of education that had kept the slaves in ignorance and made it possible for the white man to exploit them. It was why he had let his own two elder sons go to France to be educated.

Toussaint passed a law to force all the black people to go back to the plantations, as paid workers, not as slaves, and with protection against ill treatment. But he did not explain, or could not make them understand, why he was doing this. Unfortunately some of them turned against him as a result.

Besides having to ward off attacks from outside, Toussaint also had enemies inside the country. These were the mulattoes. They had white fathers and black mothers and had been well treated in the past. Many of them had been sent to Paris by their fathers to be educated. The only difference between them and the whites was that they could not hold positions of power. But they thought themselves superior to the black people, and did not want Toussaint, a black man, as

Governor of the island. So they formed themselves into an army, with a mulatto leader, against him.

However, from the ruins of the slave revolt Toussaint managed to build up a *free* country. During the next ten years he got production back to at least half of what it had been before all the devastation and in spite of all the forces working against him. Most important of all, he did this without slavery.

Chapter 4
Toussaint's Capture

St. Dominigue still remained a colony of France. What was happening there? After all the chaos of the French Revolution and the mass executions of its citizens, Napoleon came to power. At first he was fully occupied with wars in Europe, conquering one country after another with his 'invincible army.' He had no time to give his mind to what was happening in St. Dominigue. But, when things calmed down a bit, he sent out a Commissioner to find out.

The report came back to him that Toussaint was like an Emperor there. Toussaint even sent him a letter addressed to "The first of the whites from the first of the blacks." What impudence! Napoleon could not tolerate any rivals. This "gilded African," as he called Toussaint, must be put in his place. So an armed force was sent out under General Leclerc to make sure that Toussaint knew who was his master. Leclerc was married to Napoleon's sister, so he was his brother-in-law.

Toussaint found out that, in spite of the ideals of the new French Republic, Napoleon planned to bring back slavery to the island. So much for Freedom, Liberty and Equality! Toussaint knew he had been right not to trust the white man's word. So when Leclerc arrived he met an army instead of a welcome. Of course the French had better arms and Toussaint was beaten in the first battle, but he did not give in. He knew that there was an outbreak of yellow fever in the island. The French soldiers would not have built up a resistance to it and many of them would die. So he called a halt to his attack. He thought that by waiting, he would be left in control of the island, because the yellow fever would deplete Leclerc's army. In this way he hoped to avoid unnecessary slaughter - always his aim.

Leclerc could also see what was happening to his army. He was ill himself and knew that he must act quickly. Somehow he must get rid of Toussaint as soon as possible. The man was much too clever, you could never tell what he was going to do next. Leclerc wrote a letter to the Minister in France, saying:

"The Government must put him (Toussaint) in some fortress in the centre of France so that by no possibility can he escape and return to St. Dominigue where he has the power of a religious leader. You cannot keep him in a place at too great a distance from the sea nor in a place too sure."

Then he tricked Toussaint into coming to meet him to talk things over. Toussaint fell into the trap because he wanted to get things settled peacefully and without bloodshed. However, Leclerc had him arrested and sent to France to be imprisoned. Toussaint hoped he would be given a fair trial when he got to Paris so that he would be able to defend himself. His wife and three sons were put on the same ship, but once they were at sea he was not allowed to see or speak to them.

When they got to France he was taken to a fortress on a mountain from which it would have been impossible to escape. He was locked in a dungeon with one tiny window too high up for him to see out. The walls were damp and it was very cold. There was a small fireplace, but he was given only a few sticks a day to burn for heat. He had just one meal a day. He was never allowed out of the cell and he was not allowed any visitors. Also he had no books. He asked his jailer for some paper so that he could write a letter to Napoleon but he never got an answer.

As winter came on it got bitterly cold in his cell and he was used to a hot climate. He had no warm clothes or even a blanket. Then his jailer went away for four days leaving him in the charge of another man. This one never went into his cell to bring him food or wood for his fire. When the first jailer came back he found that Toussaint was dead. He was sitting beside the empty grate with his head resting against the wet wall. The verdict was that he died of a stroke and pneumonia. He was sixty years old.

When he said goodbye to his eldest son before going into imprisonment his last words were:

"When you get back to St. Dominigue you must forget that the French murdered your father."

But we must never forget him, for it was Toussaint who brought "the torch of Liberty" to his people.

After he was dead, the torch was carried on by Dessaline, another slave. He became the rebel leader. He defeated Leclerc's army because, as Toussaint had guessed, the yellow fever had taken its toll of the French soldiers. Leclerc also died. Then Dessaline proclaimed the colony of St. Dominigue an independent country on January 1st, 1804. He changed its name to Haiti. It was the first black republic in the world. Alas, Toussaint was not alive to share the victory, but without him it could not have happened.